TIME TO LEARN ABOUT
MEASURING TIME

Pam Scheunemann

Consulting Editor, Diane Craig, M.A./Reading Specialist

Published by ABDO Publishing Company, 8000 West 78th Street, Edina, Minnesota 55439.

Copyright © 2008 by Abdo Consulting Group, Inc. International copyrights reserved in all countries.

No part of this book may be reproduced in any form without written permission from the publisher. SandCastle™ is a trademark and logo of ABDO Publishing Company. Printed in the United States.

Editor: Pam Price
Content Developer: Nancy Tuminelly
Cover and Interior Design and Production: Mighty Media
Photo Credits: Brand X Pictures, ShutterStock

Library of Congress Cataloging-in-Publication Data

Scheunemann, Pam, 1955-
   Time to learn about measuring time / Pam Scheunemann.
      p. cm.
   ISBN 978-1-60453-016-2
   1. Time measurements--Juvenile literature. I. Title.
   QB213.S35 2008
   529'.7--dc22
                           2007030074

SandCastle™ Level: Fluent

SandCastle™ books are created by a team of professional educators, reading specialists, and content developers around five essential components—phonemic awareness, phonics, vocabulary, text comprehension, and fluency—to assist young readers as they develop reading skills and strategies and increase their general knowledge. All books are written, reviewed, and leveled for guided reading, early reading intervention, and Accelerated Reader® programs for use in shared, guided, and independent reading and writing activities to support a balanced approach to literacy instruction. The SandCastle™ series has four levels that correspond to early literacy development. The levels are provided to help teachers and parents select appropriate books for young readers.

Emerging Readers
(no flags)

Beginning Readers
(1 flag)

Transitional Readers
(2 flags)

Fluent Readers
(3 flags)

SandCastle™ would like to hear from you. Please send us your comments and suggestions.
sandcastle@abdopublishing.com

time

Time is an interesting thing. You can't touch it. You can't see it. You can't hold it. But it is always passing by!

Let's learn about measuring time.

time

3

People in the past used the changing positions of the sun, moon, and stars to make different kinds of calendars.

time fact

The Maya lived in Central America and Mexico. The calendars they developed almost 2,000 years ago were very accurate.

We use a calendar to measure the months, weeks, and days in a year.

time fact

Many of the ideas from ancient calendars led to the calendar that we use today.

JANUARY

SUN	MON	TUE	WED	THU	FRI	SAT
	1	2	3	4	5	6
7	8	9	10	11	12	13
4	15	16	17	18	19	20
1	22	23	24	25	26	27
8	29	30	31			

FEBRUARY

SUN	MON	TUE	WED	THU	FRI	SAT
				1	2	3
4	5	6	7	8	9	10
11	12	13	14	15	16	17
18	19	20	21	22	23	24
25	26	27	28			

MARCH

SUN	MON	TUE	WED	THU	FRI	SAT
4	5	6	7			
11	12	13	14			
18	19	20	21	22		
25	26	27	28	29		

APRIL

SUN	MON	TUE	WED	THU	FRI	SAT
1	2	3	4	5	6	7
8	9	10	11	12	13	14
5	16	17	18	19	20	21
2	23	24	25	26	27	28
9	30					

MAY

SUN	MON	TUE	WED	THU	FRI	SAT
		1	2	3	4	5
6	7	8	9	10	11	12
13	14	15	16	17	18	19
20	21	22	23	24	25	26
27	28	29	30	31		

JUNE

SUN	MON	TUE	WED	THU	FRI	SAT
					1	2
3	4	5	6	7	8	9
10	11	12	13	14	15	16
17	18	19	20	21	22	23
24	25	26	27	28	29	30

JULY

SUN	MON	TUE	WED	THU	FRI	SAT
	1	2	3	4	5	6
8	9	10	11	12	13	14
5	16	17	18	19	20	21
2	23	24	25	26	27	28
9	30	31				

AUGUST

SUN	MON	TUE	WED	THU	FRI	SAT
			1	2	3	4
5	6	7	8	9	10	11
12	13	14	15	16	17	18
19	20	21	22	23	24	25
26	27	28	29	30	31	

SEPTEMBER

SUN	MON	TUE	WED	THU	FRI	SAT
						1
2	3	4	5	6	7	8
9	10	11	12	13	14	15
16	17	18	19	20	21	22
23	24	25	26	27	28	29
30						

OCTOBER

SUN	MON	TUE	WED	THU	FRI	SAT
	1	2	3	4	5	6
7	8	9	10	11	12	13
4	15	16	17	18	19	20
1	22	23	24	25	26	27
8	29	30	31			

NOVEMBER

SUN	MON	TUE	WED	THU	FRI	SAT
				1	2	3
4	5	6	7	8	9	10
11	12	13	14	15	16	17
18	19	20	21	22	23	24
25	26	27	28	29	30	

D...

SUN	MON	TUE	WED	THU		
2	3	4	5			
9	10	11	12			
16	17	18	1			
23	24	25				
30	31					

Early clocks were based on the sun's movement. They included the shadow clock and the sundial. Sundials are still used today, but mostly for decoration.

time fact

Clocks were invented so people could measure time during a day.

Hourglasses and sandglasses measure time. There are large hourglasses that measure an hour. There are small sandglasses that measure only a minute.

time fact

People started using things such as candles, sand, and water to measure time without using the sun.

Mechanical clocks were developed to keep time more accurately. They could also be made small enough for people to carry around with them.

Mechanical clocks have gears inside that make the clock's hands move. People wind them to tighten the spring that turns the gears.

clocks

A clock that tells the hours, minutes, and seconds using hands is called an analog clock. The small hand points toward the hour. The long hand points toward the minutes. The very thin hand shows the seconds.

time fact

On an analog clock, the hours are indicated by either numbers or dashes.

A digital clock shows the time without hands. It uses numbers separated by a colon. The hour is shown on the left side. The minutes are shown on the right side.

Digital clocks can be very big or very small. Tiny digital clocks can even be put on key chains!

time fact

In 1883, the owners of the railroads in the United States established a Standard Time System. This made scheduling trains easier. Before then, each town set its own local time.

time fact

The railroads' Standard Time System was made into law when the U.S. Congress passed the Standard Time Act in 1918.

The earth has 24 time zones. Each time zone is one hour different from the zones next to it. Knowing about time zones is helpful when traveling or making long-distance phone calls.

Times zones are divided by meridians. The meridian in Greenwich, England, is the starting point for every time zone in the world.

time
fact

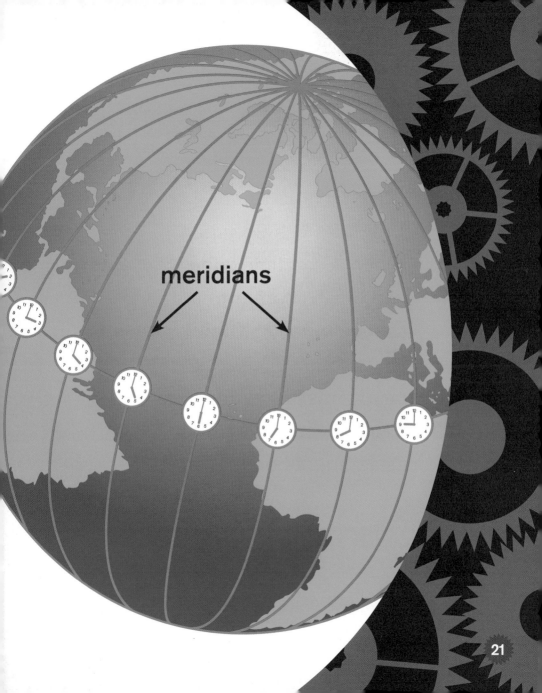

meridians

There are many different ways to measure time. How do you measure time?

Do you wear a watch? Have you ever used a sandglass? Do you keep track of activities and assignments on a calendar?

The official U.S. time is kept by the National Institute of Standards and Technology (NIST) and the U.S. Naval Observatory (USNO).